You Can Be

POKéMON
Master Artist!

Gotta catch 'em all!

by Ron Zalme

Troll

Special thanks to Susan Eisner and Christine Kelly.

A Creative Media Applications Production

Art Direction by Fabia Wargin Design

You Can Be a Pokémon Master Artist!

Gotta Draw 'em All! Here's how:

It takes great patience and practice to rise to the rank of Pokémon Master. Along the way you'll make some mistakes and experience some setbacks. But in the end, if you persevere, you'll reach your goal. The same is true of becoming a Pokémon Master Artist. You'll need patience and practice, and you'll learn from your mistakes. That's where this book can help you. We'll teach you, step by step, how to draw Mankey, Jigglypuff, Weedle, and many other Pokémon. In the end, if you stay with it, you will become a Pokémon Master Artist.

Don't worry if your drawings aren't perfect the first time. A Pokémon trainer doesn't always win his or her first battle. Keep practicing! In this book, you'll learn how to draw facial expressions, bodies, and Pokémon in motion. Soon you'll be making up—*and illustrating*—your own exciting Pokémon adventures. Here are a few things you should know before getting started:

1. Draw lightly as you sketch. You'll have plenty of time to darken your lines as you finish your drawing and fill in the details.

2. Stay loose! Let your hand and arm move freely. Don't grip your pencil like you're Onix trying to crush an opponent! Drawing should be relaxing and fun.

3. Don't worry about mistakes—that's why erasers were invented!

4. Practice, and be patient. It takes time to get good at drawing.

I CHOOSE YOU...to begin your quest to be a Pokémon Master Artist!

MATERIALS
medium pencil
eraser
8 1/2" x 11" (21.5 x 28 cm) sheets of white paper

Here are the basic shapes you can use to draw everything in this book.

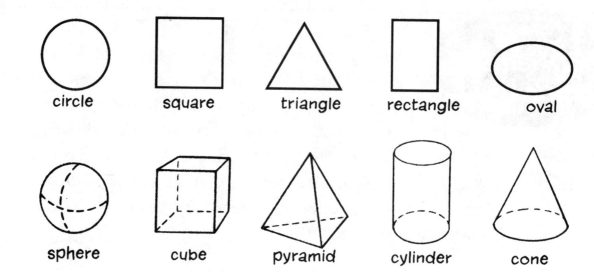

circle   square   triangle   rectangle   oval

sphere   cube   pyramid   cylinder   cone

All you can really draw with your pencil on a piece of paper are two-dimensional flat shapes, like the five basic shapes in the top row above. Part of the magic of drawing is learning how to create the illusion of three-dimensional objects on your two-dimensional piece of paper. Look at the circle above. It's round and two-dimensional. Now pick up a ball. It's also round, but it's three-dimensional, a real object. The trick to drawing believable characters is to create the illusion on paper that what you are looking at is three-dimensional (like the ball, or a Pokémon), even though it is really only two-dimensional (like the circle). Each of the two-dimensional shapes in the top row above has a three-dimensional "partner" just below it. Simply by adding two crisscrossing dotted lines to the circle, you create the illusion of its three-dimensional partner, the sphere. The same is true for each of the shapes on this page. Practice drawing the two-dimensional basic shapes, then move on to the 3-D shapes like the cube, pyramid, etc. Now you're ready to try your first Pokémon. Let's begin with **Jigglypuff!**

Step 1.

Start by drawing a large circle for Jigglypuff's head/body (1). Next, add crisscrossing guidelines (A & B) to the circle, dividing it in half horizontally and vertically. These guidelines are there to help you place the elements that follow. Now draw two smaller circles (2) for the eyes, placing them on guideline "A." Add an oval (3), centered on the forehead, for Jigglypuff's curl of hair. Finally, draw two same-sized triangles (4) to make the ears.

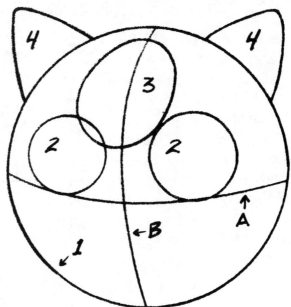

Step 2.

Add details to the eyes, curl, ears, and top of the head. Then draw the mouth, hands, and feet, as shown.

Step 3.

Fill in the ears with black. Finish your drawing by darkening the lines you want to keep and erasing the lines you don't need. Jigglypuff is ready to sing its enemies to sleep!

Step 1.

Start Chansey off with a large egg-shaped body (1). Add the crisscrossing guidelines (A & B). Note that the "A" guideline is near the top of Chansey's body. These lines will help you place the character's features (eyes, mouth, hands, etc.). Sketch an oval shape (2) on guideline "B." Now add two banana shapes (3) on each side of the head for Chansey's hair. Finish up the first step by drawing in the feet (4).

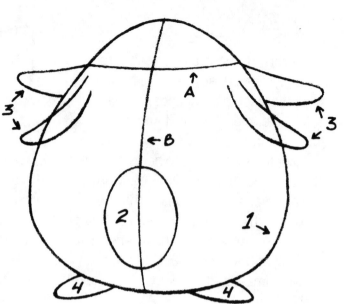

Step 2.

Add the eyes, mouth, and chin line, using the guidelines to help you place them. Now draw a third hair shape on each side of the head, plus Chansey's hands, tail, and pouch, as shown.

Step 3.

Blacken the eyes, leaving white highlights at the top. Then darken the lines you want to keep, and erase the extra lines. Chansey is ready to use its magical powers!

Step 1.

Begin with a circle (1) for Doduo's body. Then draw two smaller circles (2) above the body. These will be Doduo's heads. Notice how one head is higher than the other. Add a horizontal guideline (A) to each circle "2," and draw a small circle and semicircle on each line "A" to form the eyes. Finish the basics by connecting the heads to the body, using curved lines, as shown, and by sketching two upside-down "Y" shapes to form the legs and feet.

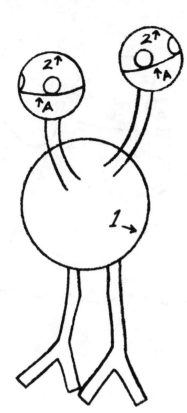

Step 2.

Add the beaks and toes, as shown. Now it's time to fluff out Doduo's feathers. Draw loosely zigzagging lines around the head and body shapes to give this Pokémon a feathery, bird-like look.

Step 3.

Fill in the eyes with black (leaving a small white highlight in each eye). Then darken the lines you want to keep, and erase the extra lines. Doduo is ready to race off at top speed!

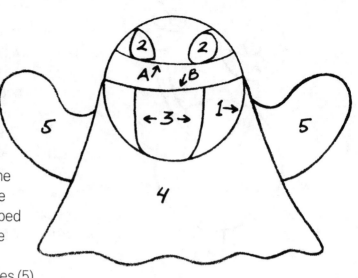

Step 1.

Once again, begin with a large circle (1), this time for Grimer's head. Draw two horizontal guidelines (A & B) across the circle. Line "A" will help you place the eyes, and line "B" will form the top of the mouth. Draw the two eye shapes (2), then outline the mouth (3). Grimer's body (4) is shaped like the bottom of a triangle. Notice the long wavy line at the base. To complete step 1, add the arm shapes (5).

Step 2.

Now add in the details. Using wavy lines to create a ghostly effect, outline the jaw, tongue, upper lip, body, and arms. Don't forget the dots for the pupils.

Step 3.

Finally, fill in the mouth with black, as shown. Darken the lines you want to keep, and erase the extra lines. Grimer is all set to suck up some sludge! Yum!

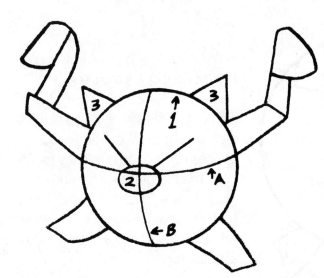

Step 1.

Begin with a large circle (1) for Mankey's head/body. Divide it with crisscrossing guidelines (A & B). These guidelines are there to help you place the elements that follow. Draw a small oval (2) at the point where the guidelines meet, to form the nose. Extend two lines out from this oval, as shown, to start the eyes. Add two triangles (3) at the top of the circle for the ears. Then add the remaining shapes, as you see here, to form Mankey's arms and legs.

Step 2.

Outline Mankey's furry body, using jagged lines, as shown. Next, add details to the eyes, nose, and ears. Complete the arms, hands, and legs, then add the feet and a long curly tail.

Step 3.

Blacken the pupils (this time leaving white on either side of each eye). Darken the lines you want to keep, and erase the extra lines. Mankey is ready to unleash a powerful Pokémon punch!

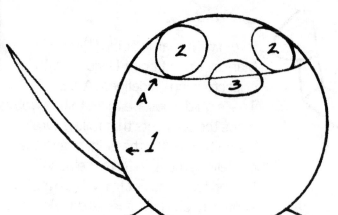

Step 1.

A large circle (1) forms Poliwag's head/body. Draw a curved horizontal guideline (A) near the top of the circle. The guideline will help you place the elements that follow. Now add the eye shapes (2). Notice how they touch both the top of the circle and guideline "A." Next, draw an oval (3) for the nose right on line "A." Add the feet shapes (4) and a long pointed tail, as shown.

Step 2.

Start at one side of Poliwag's nose and draw a large circular shape for its mouth. Notice that the shape ends at the other side of the nose. Now add a thick black swirl within the circular mouth shape. Be careful—don't let the swirl line touch itself at any point. Complete this step by adding details to the eyes, nose, head, and tail, as shown.

Step 3.

Finish your drawing by filling in the pupils with black, leaving white highlights, as shown. Darken the lines you want to keep, and erase the extra lines. Poliwag is ready to go for a swim!

Step 1.

Start with a large circle (1) for Weedle's head. Add a curved horizontal guideline (A) near the top of the circle. The guideline will help you position the eyes. Now start adding smaller, overlapping circles (2-8) that extend down and curve to the right.

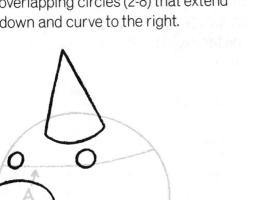

Step 2.

Place a cone shape on top of the head for Weedle's stinger. Add two small circles for the eyes and an oval for the nose. Next, draw a small circle in each of the body sections and three half-circles outside sections 2, 3, and 4. Finally, add the little shape at the end of Weedle's body, as shown.

Step 3.

Fill in the eyes with black, leaving white highlights. Don't forget to blacken the circle at the end of Weedle's body as well. Then darken the lines you want to keep, and erase the extra lines. Watch out for Weedle's poisonous stinger!

Step 1.

Start Slowpoke off with a large head oval (1). Then draw a larger, overlapping oval (2) for the body. Add two small ovals (3) to the top of the head to form the ears. Slowpoke's mouth is made up of two semicircular shapes (4 & 5). To complete step 1, add the tail (6), using two long, sweeping curves.

Step 2.

Next, add the eyes and details to the ear and mouth. Don't forget the nostrils and the two teeth. Complete this step by drawing the legs and feet, as shown. Notice the back leg curves off the back of the body oval.

Step 3.

There's nothing to blacken on Slowpoke—its eyes stay white except for a little black dot in the center of each one. Darken the lines you want to keep, and erase any extra ones. Slowpoke is all set to stay right where it is. This Pokémon hates to move!

Step 1.

Begin with a medium-sized circle (1) for the head. Draw a curved horizontal guideline (A) in the lower part of this circle. Then, using the guideline to help you, add an oval (2) for Dratini's big nose and the two eye shapes (3). The curving body shape (4) is much larger than the head. Add the ear shapes (5) to the top of the head.

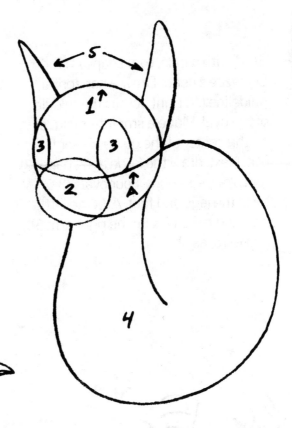

Step 2.

Draw a small circle on Dratini's forehead, then add details to the ears, face, and body, as shown. Finally, draw three curved lines to form the end of the tail.

Step 3.

Add black to the eyes (leaving white highlights), as shown. Finish up by darkening the lines you want to keep and erasing any extra lines. Dratini is ready to dive underwater!

13

Step 1.

Start with a long, oval shape (1) for Drowzee's head. Draw a horizontal guideline (A) right across the middle of the oval. Place a small semicircle on the center of the guideline for the eye. Next, draw the large egg shape (2) for Drowzee's body. Four ovals (3-6) form the legs and feet. Add the left arm and hand (7 & 8), the right arm (9), and ears, as shown.

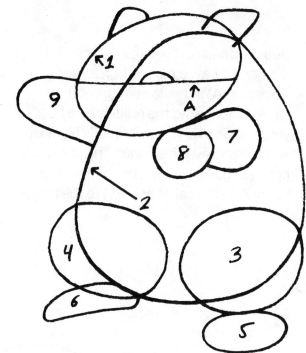

Step 2.

Now draw the droopy snout coming off the head oval and add the crease lines going across it. Fill in the remaining details on the head, arm, hands, legs, and feet. Don't forget the wavy line across the mid-section.

Step 3.

Darken the lines you want to keep, and erase any extra lines. Drowzee is ready to gobble down his opponent's dreams!

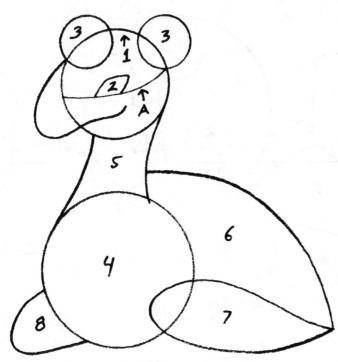

Step 1.

Start with a circle (1) for the head. Divide the circle with a curved guideline (A). Now place the eye shape (2) on the guideline, about in the center. Two smaller circles (3) form the ears. Draw a larger circle (4) below the head, leaving some space in between. Connect the two circles with the neck shape (5). Lapras' body (6) extends out from the neck in a long curved line. Add the flippers (7 & 8) and a curved snout to the head, as shown.

Step 2.

Next, add details to the head, body, and flippers. Notice the bumps on Lapras' back and the point extending out from its forehead.

Step 3.

Complete the final details by adding the body spots and wrinkle lines, then blackening the eye, as shown. Notice how half the eye is white and half is black, but the black section has a white dot inside it. Finally, darken the lines you want to keep, and erase any extra lines. Lapras is now ready to carry passengers across small bodies of water!

Step 1.

A large circle (1) forms Geodude's head/body. Draw crisscrossing guidelines (A & B). These guidelines are there to help you place the elements that follow. Begin with the eye shapes (2) on guideline "A." Then form the mouth with a curved line (3) at the bottom of the head circle. Next, two rectangular shapes on either side of the head (4) form the arms. Add the two fist shapes (5) at the ends of the arms. Draw Geodude's eyebrow line, as shown, and you've completed step 1.

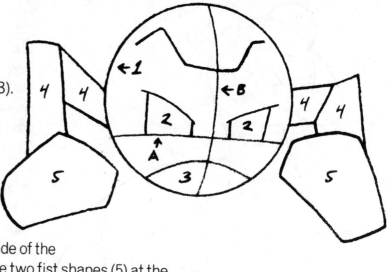

Step 2.

Give Geodude a rocky look by drawing angular lines along the outside of the head/body circle. Add the arm muscles and facial details, and draw the fingers.

Step 3.

Blacken the eyes (being sure to leave white highlights). Then darken the lines you want to keep, and erase the extra lines. Be careful—don't trip over Geodude as he sits motionless in a field, trying his best to look like a rock!

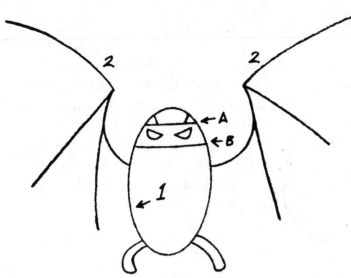

Step 1.

Start Golbat off with a medium-sized oval (1). Add two horizontal guidelines (A & B) close to the top of the oval. These guidelines are there to help you place the elements that follow. Draw the two eye shapes in between the guidelines. Then form the ears with two short lines above guideline "A." Begin the wings by adding four longer lines (2) to each side of the body. To complete this step, add the two curved legs, as shown.

Step 2.

Outline Golbat's wide-open mouth in a long "U" shape. Add some curved lines around the lines you drew in step 1 to complete the wings. Then add feet and four pointed fangs. Don't forget the eye and ear details.

Step 3.

Finally, fill in the mouth with black, being careful to leave the fangs white. Darken the lines you want to keep, and erase any extra lines. Watch out! Don't let Golbat bite!

GROWLITHE

Step 1.

Begin with a head oval (1). Divide it with a horizontal guideline (A) near the top. On the middle of the guideline, add a small triangle (2) to form the eye, then add the ear and nose, as shown. The body (3) is bean-shaped. Draw an overlapping oval (4) for the tail, and the leg shape (5).

Step 2.

Add the remaining details to the face, legs, and feet. Then use zigzagging lines for the fur on Growlithe's head, chest, and tail, as shown.

Step 3.

Fill in the pupil and nose with black, leaving a white highlight in each. Add zigzagging stripes to the body and legs, as you see here. Then darken the lines you want to keep, and clean up your extra lines. Growlithe is ready to bark at and bite strangers!

Step 1.

Haunter's head is a big circle (1). Divide the head horizontally and vertically with crisscrossing guidelines (A & B). These guidelines are there to help you place the elements that follow. Draw two triangle shapes (2) for the eyes on guideline "A." Add two larger triangles (3) on top of the head to form the ears. The tail shape (4) is made up of two curved lines that come together at a point. Add the hand shapes (5), and you're done with step 1.

Step 2.

Next, add Haunter's evil, toothy grin, just under guideline "A." Fill in the eye details. Then add zigzagging lines to each side of the head and the tail. Finally, complete the hands by drawing fingers and claws, as shown.

Step 3.

Just darken the lines you want to keep and erase any extra lines, and Haunter is ready to scare all who cross its path!

Step 1.

Begin with a large circle (1) to form Horsea's head. Draw a horizontal guideline (A) near the bottom of the circle. Add the nose shape (2) and two ovals (3) for the eyes. Now draw the body shape (4). Overlap a smaller circle (5) at the bottom of the body. Finish step 1 by adding three spikes to the head, as shown.

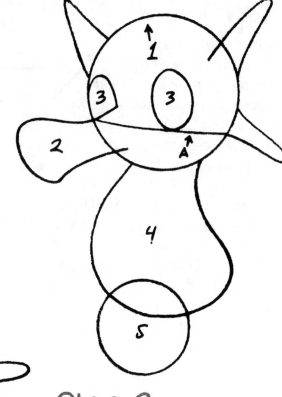

Step 2.

Add details to the eyes and a small oval to the end of the nose. Draw two more head spikes, as shown, and Horsea's fin on its back. Add the remaining details to the tail and body, including the stripes on the chest.

Step 3.

Blacken the opening in the nose, then darken the lines you want to keep, and erase any extra lines. Horsea is ready to blast an opponent with a burst of ink!

Step 1.

Start Jolteon off with a circle (1) for its head. Draw a curved horizontal guideline (A) through the center of the circle. Place the eye shape (2) on the guideline. Then add the snout (3) and the ear shape (4). The body shape (5) comes next. Draw it as you see here. To complete step 1, outline the pointed tail and the legs, as shown.

Step 2.

Add lots of zigzagging spikes to give Jolteon that electrified look. Draw the other two legs, as shown, and fill in the remaining details on the head and feet.

Step 3.

Blacken the eye, leaving a small white highlight. Then darken the lines you want to keep, and erase the extra lines. Jolteon is ready to zap any opponent!

Step 1.

Start with a small circle (1) for the head. Add a horizontal guideline (A) near the bottom of the circle. Place the two eye shapes on the guideline, then add a small triangle on top of the head. Next, draw a semicircle (2) to form Dragonite's snout. The body (3) is an unusual shape. Draw it as you see here. Then add the tail (4), arms (5), feet (6), and wings (7). These are also unusual shapes, so practice them separately, then add them to your drawing.

Step 2.

Use curved lines to form the antennae on top of Dragonite's head. Then fill in the details on the face, arm, and legs. Use cone shapes for the claws, as shown. Complete the wings, and add stripes to the body and tail.

Step 3.

Blacken the eyes (being sure to leave white highlights). Then darken the lines you want to keep, and erase any extra lines. Now watch Dragonite soar!

Step 1.

Begin by drawing a circle (1) for the head. Add a horizontal guideline (A) in the lower portion of the circle. Place the eye shape (2) on the guideline, then draw the ear shape (3). Flareon's nose (4) is small and sits on the outside of the head circle. Now draw the body shapes (5 & 6), legs (7), and tail (8). Add a curl of hair on top of the head circle, and you're done with step 1.

Step 2.

Complete the first ear, and outline a second ear behind it. Then add details to the curl, face, body, and legs, as shown. Jagged lines form the fur. Use them to give Flareon a fuzzy look.

Step 3.

Blacken the eye (being careful to leave a white highlight), then darken the lines you want to keep, and erase any extra lines. Flareon is ready to heat things up!

Step 1.

Start with a large circle for the head (1). Draw two crisscrossing guidelines (A & B), dividing the circle vertically and horizontally. These guidelines are there to help you place the elements that follow. Add two triangle shapes for the eyes (2) on guideline "A" and a squiggly line for the mouth on guideline "B." Now draw a larger, overlapping circle (3) for the body. Copy the ear shapes (4 & 5), then outline the legs and foot, as shown.

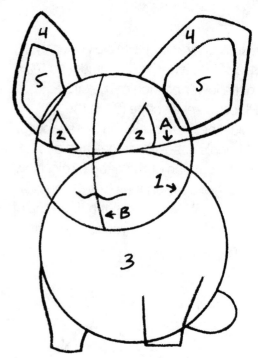

Step 2.

Next, add details to the ears, face, body, and feet, as shown. Don't forget Nidoran's sharp spikes and bucktooth.

Step 3.

Just add the body spots, and you're done. Darken the lines you want to keep, and erase the extra lines. Watch out for those poisonous spikes sticking out from Nidoran's cheeks!

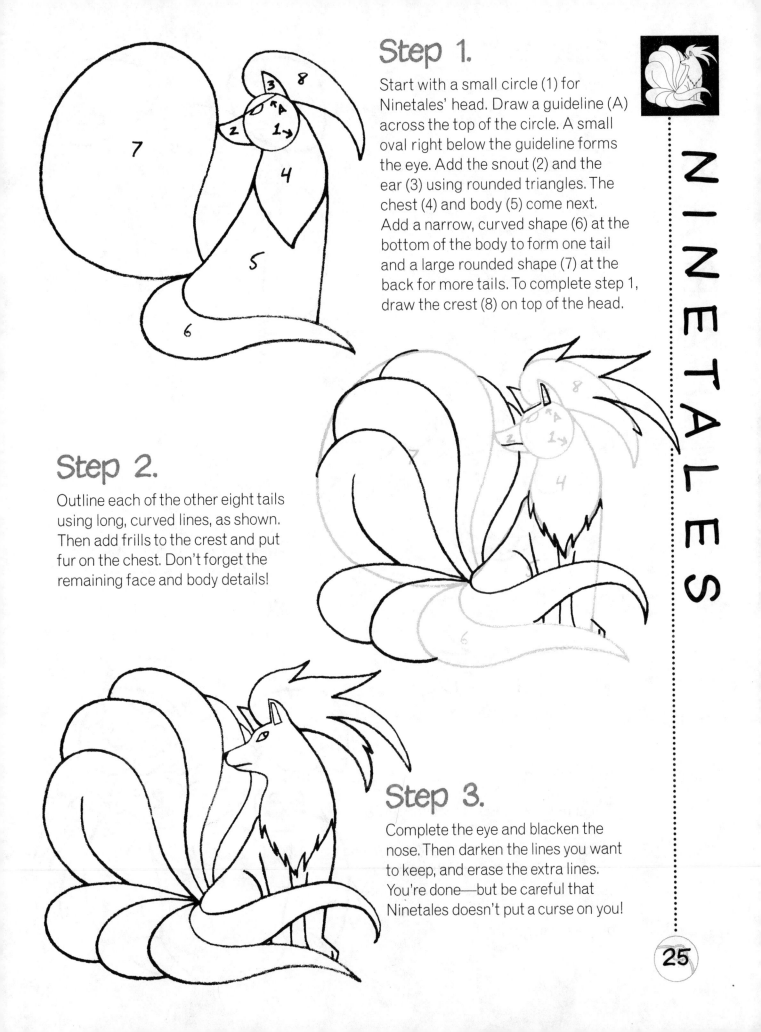

Step 1.

Start with a small circle (1) for Ninetales' head. Draw a guideline (A) across the top of the circle. A small oval right below the guideline forms the eye. Add the snout (2) and the ear (3) using rounded triangles. The chest (4) and body (5) come next. Add a narrow, curved shape (6) at the bottom of the body to form one tail and a large rounded shape (7) at the back for more tails. To complete step 1, draw the crest (8) on top of the head.

Step 2.

Outline each of the other eight tails using long, curved lines, as shown. Then add frills to the crest and put fur on the chest. Don't forget the remaining face and body details!

Step 3.

Complete the eye and blacken the nose. Then darken the lines you want to keep, and erase the extra lines. You're done—but be careful that Ninetales doesn't put a curse on you!

Step 1.

Start off with an oval (1) for Paras' head/body. Draw crisscrossing guidelines (A & B) in the oval. These guidelines are there to help you place the elements that follow. Add two circles (2) for the eyes on guideline "A." Draw a small oval (3) for the mouth, with an even smaller oval (4) inside it. Then outline the mushroom shapes (5) at the top and the claw shapes (6) below.

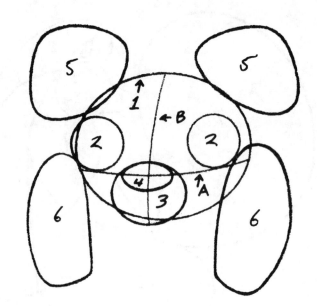

Step 2.

Next, add details to the eyes, mouth, and head, as shown. Don't forget the five tiny circles between the eyes. Draw the legs on each side of the head, and two cone shapes for Paras' sharp claws.

Step 3.

Finish up by adding spots to the mushrooms on Paras' head. Then fill in the eyes and mouth with black, as shown. Darken the lines you want to keep, and erase the extra ones, and Paras is ready to burrow underground!

Step 1.

Begin drawing Persian with a circle (1) for its head. Divide the circle with crisscrossing guidelines (A & B). These guidelines are there to help you place the elements that follow. Add the eye shapes (2) on guideline "A." Then draw the mouth and tongue (3) and the two ear shapes (4) on top of the head. Don't forget the curved lines on the sides of the head as well. The body (5) is a large bean shape, and the legs (6, 7, & 8) are made up of long, curved lines.

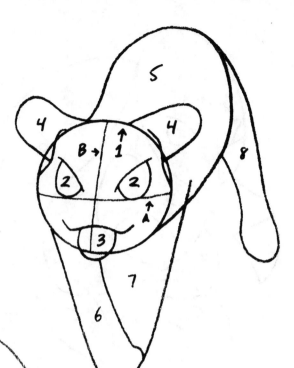

Step 2.

Draw a small circle in the center of Persian's forehead. Then add details to the ears, eyes, nose, mouth, and jaw. Draw three long whiskers on each side of the face. Finally, complete the details on the body, leg, and feet, and add a long, curly tail, as shown.

Step 3.

Blacken the outer edges of Persian's ears, then darken the lines you want to keep, and erase the extra lines. This Pokémon is ready to pounce!

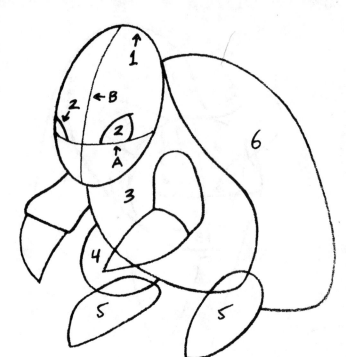

Step 1.

Start with an oval (1) for Sandslash's head. Divide the oval with criss-crossing guidelines (A & B). These guidelines are there to help you place the elements that follow. Add the eye shapes (2) on guideline "A." Next, draw the large, bean-shaped body (3). Add a semicircle (4) to form the right leg and two pointed ovals (5) for the feet. Draw a long, curved line (6) to guide you in placing the back spikes. Then add the arms and claw shapes, as shown.

Step 2.

Draw lots of armored spikes on Sandslash's back and head, as shown. Then add details to the face, arms, claws, body, and feet.

Step 3.

Blacken the eyes (being sure to leave some white highlights), then darken the lines you want to keep, and erase the extra lines. Now Sandslash is ready to unleash a fury swipe!

Step 1.

Start with an oval (1) for Abra's head. Draw crisscrossing guidelines (A & B) and add the eye-slit lines extending up from guideline "A." Draw triangles (2) for the ears (notice the left triangle is a little smaller and sits lower on the head than the right) and a smaller oval (3) for the body. Divide the body oval in half with a curved horizontal line. Add the arm shapes (4 & 5) next, then draw the legs and feet, as you see here. Complete this step by drawing a long, curved tail (6) and adding Abra's rounded shoulders (7).

Step 2.

Add angled lines to the face and ears and two short lines for the nostrils. Then draw the hand, leg, and feet details, as shown. Copy the shapes on the body and shoulders to create the suite of armor. Don't forget the two curved stripes on Abra's tail.

Step 3.

Blacken the underside of the armor, as shown. Then darken the lines you want to keep, and erase the extra lines, and Abra is ready to send out powerful brain waves!

Step 1.

Start with a circle (1) for Lickitung's head. Draw a horizontal guideline (A) near the top of the circle. Place a tiny circle (2) on the guideline to form the right eye, and two semicircles (3) on the outside of the head oval for the left eye and the nose. Next, draw a slightly smaller circle (4), connecting it to the head with a long, curved line, as shown. The body (5) is bean-shaped. Add the tail shape (6) at the back of the body. Finish step 1 by outlining the arms and legs, as shown.

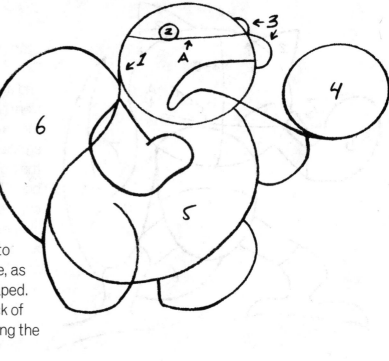

Step 2.

Use curved lines to complete Lickitung's long, curled tongue. Then add stripes to the belly and draw the knee circles, as shown. Add the final details to the hands, feet, and tail. Don't forget the two short lines for the nostrils.

Step 3.

Blacken the eyes, leaving a white highlight in each. Then darken the lines you want to keep, and erase the extra lines. Lickitung's ready for a tongue lashing!

Step 1.

A medium-sized oval (1) forms Mew's head. Draw two crisscrossing guidelines (A & B) to divide the oval vertically and horizontally. These guidelines are there to help you place the elements that follow. Place the eye shapes (2) on guideline "A." Add two triangle shapes (3) to the top of the head to form the ears. Draw another oval (4) below the head oval, leaving a little space in between the two shapes. Connect the ovals with the neck shape (5). Then add the arms and feet, as shown. Notice how much smaller the arms are than the feet.

Step 2.

Add details to the eyes, cheeks, mouth, hands, belly, and feet. Then draw a long, curving tail with an oval shape at the tip, as shown.

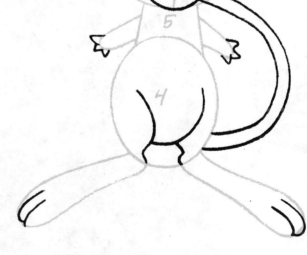

Step 3.

Darken the lines you want to keep, and erase any extra lines. Meet the newest Pokémon!